Who Was
Pete Seeger?

by Noel MacCarry

illustrated by Stephen Marchesi

Grosset & Dunlap
An Imprint of Penguin Random House

For Debbie, Brian, Erin, Kevin,
and Bridget—NM

GROSSET & DUNLAP
Penguin Young Readers Group
An Imprint of Penguin Random House LLC

Text copyright © 2017 by Noel MacCarry. Illustrations copyright © 2017 by Penguin Random House LLC. All rights reserved.
Published by Grosset & Dunlap, an imprint of Penguin Random House LLC, 345 Hudson Street, New York, New York 10014. The WHO HQ™ colophon and GROSSET & DUNLAP are trademarks of Penguin Random House LLC. Printed in the USA.

Library of Congress Cataloging-in-Publication Data is available.

ISBN 9780448484754 (paperback)   10 9 8 7 6 5 4 3 2 1
ISBN 9780515157987 (library binding)   10 9 8 7 6 5 4 3 2 1

Contents

Who Was Pete Seeger? 1

Young Peter 4

Finding His Way 18

Love and War 42

Little House on the Hudson 56

Pete on Trial 68

We Shall Overcome 77

Give Peace a Chance 85

The Clearwater 89

American Hero 96

Timelines 106

Bibliography 108

Contents

Who Was Pete Seeger?

Madison Square Garden was packed with more than fifteen thousand fans. It was May 3, 2009. Everyone had come to honor a very tall, very thin, plainly dressed musician. His name was Pete Seeger and it was his ninetieth birthday.

Pete who? Is that what you are asking yourself?

Although he wrote and performed songs that all of America knows and loves, many young people today don't recognize his name. That's because for many years, his voice was banned from radio, and he was never seen on television.

That night, however, fans were thanking him for both his music and his courage to stand up for his beliefs. His belief that all people are equal, no matter the color of their skin. His belief that we must protect nature. His belief that peace on earth is possible.

At Madison Square Garden, rock and folk music legends performed in Pete's honor. They included Bruce Springsteen, Dave Matthews, and Joan Baez. Near the end, all the stars and the audience joined hands while singing "We Shall Overcome." Pete helped make that song a rallying

cry during the 1960s when African Americans struggled so hard for equal rights.

Singing songs for freedom was the story of Pete Seeger's long life.

CHAPTER 1
Young Peter

Peter Seeger was born in New York City on May 3, 1919. (He wasn't known as "Pete" until much later.) His parents, Charles and Constance, were musicians. Charles wrote classical music and taught in universities. Constance was a talented violinist. Peter had two older brothers.

Charles Jr. was seven years older. He grew up to become a famous astronomer. John, five years older, became a well-known teacher.

Peter was eighteen months old when Charles and Constance took the family on an unusual adventure. They packed a piano and their belongings in a homemade trailer. It looked like a covered wagon. Charles hitched the trailer to his Model T Ford and headed to the South.

RHODE ISLAND
MASSACHUSETTS
CONNECTICUT
NEW YORK

New York City

PENNSYLVANIA
Philadelphia

NEW JERSEY

DELAWARE
MARYLAND

Washington, DC

Richmond
VIRGINIA

Raleigh
NORTH CAROLINA

The Seegers hoped to bring classical music—
the music of composers like Mozart and

Beethoven—to country folks. The trailer had a stage that pulled out for performances.

Life on the road was difficult. Dirt roads turned to mud when it rained. Peter's mother had to boil water over a campfire to wash his diapers. After Peter almost stumbled into the fire, his mother

said, "Charlie, this is not going to work."

Charles agreed.

The family had made it as far as North Carolina. Audiences listened with curiosity to the classical concerts. But country people had their own music. They played fiddles, banjos, and guitars. When Charles Seeger heard them, he became more interested in their folk music than they were in *his* music. The Seegers packed up and returned to New York.

Unfortunately, Charles no longer had a teaching job, and things became tense between Peter's parents.

Peter's mother and father decided to live apart and in time they got a divorce. As for the boys, they spent summer vacations with their father in Patterson, New York, at their grandparents' house. Each night, Peter and his brothers slept with their father in the barn that was next to the main house.

On the long summer afternoons, Peter explored the woods nearby. For him, it was heaven.

On visits to his mother, Peter found musical instruments all around the house. Pretty soon Peter taught himself songs on the organ, accordion, marimba, and more. Peter liked learning music by ear rather than by reading notes. His mother tried to teach him piano. Peter didn't like sitting still, and the lessons bored him.

Besides music, Peter loved reading. His favorite books were by Ernest Thompson Seton, who founded the Boy Scouts. Seton wrote outdoor adventures. His characters knew how to hunt, track wildlife, and survive in the woods. Peter wanted to be like them. At his grandparents' home, Peter would dress up like a Native American Indian. He even built his own sixteen-foot-high tepee.

At thirteen, Peter was sent to a boys' boarding school in Avon, Connecticut. Peter was a bright student and a good writer. His love of nature grew deeper at Avon, where he worked helping to blaze trails in the thousands of wooded acres owned by the school.

At Avon, a music teacher let him try out a four-string banjo. Right away, Peter fell in love with the instrument. His music teacher said he could buy the banjo for ten dollars.

Peter wrote to his mother pleading for the money. At first she ignored his request. But when another letter from Peter came weeks later, still asking, "Please, Mother, can I have that banjo?" she gave in.

Soon Peter was playing his banjo in the school jazz band. He liked the popular music of the time, including Dixieland jazz with its strong beat. He also liked the music of the great Gershwin brothers, George and Ira.

Peter's father married again. Charles and his new wife, Ruth, became big fans of American folk music. So after Peter's high school graduation in 1936, his father took him south on another musical road trip.

The trip opened Peter's ears and changed his life forever. In the Appalachian Mountains of North Carolina, Peter heard people play the five-string banjo. It was foot-stomping music! Nothing like it was played on the radio stations

Peter listened to. Back then, America was listening to big jazz bands led by musicians like Benny Goodman and Tommy Dorsey. Bing Crosby was a top singer in those days.

For Pete Seeger, however, folk music—and the banjo—would become his life's calling.

American Roots Music

In colonial days, classical music from Europe was favored. However, by the twentieth century, new kinds of music had grown popular—music that was distinctly American, including folk, jazz, and the blues. This American music arose from the different races and groups living in the United States.

Folk music came from the mountain states of the South. Black Americans created the blues and jazz. Blues music originally expressed the pain and suffering of African American slaves.

All of this music came from the experiences of ordinary people—love, work, pain, poverty, and joy.

CHAPTER 2
Finding His Way

After the summer road trip, Peter entered Harvard University. Peter was able to get a scholarship that paid part of the cost of school. He also had a job as a waiter.

At Harvard, Peter became known as "Pete." The name suited him. But Harvard University did not. The classes bored him. He wanted to learn newspaper reporting, but nothing like that was taught at Harvard. He read a lot, just not the books for his classes. He also joined the Banjo Club.

Pete entered college in 1936, during the Great Depression. Nearly one out of every four Americans had lost his or her job by 1932. Hundreds of thousands were homeless. People stood in long lines to get a little free bread or soup.

Even those with jobs didn't have it easy. A six-day workweek with ten-hour days was not uncommon. Workers often took whatever pay was offered, no matter how low.

At Harvard, Pete joined a group of students trying to improve working people's lives. The group—the Young Communists—believed that America needed a different kind of government to make that happen. It admired the government of the Soviet Union—Communism.

Communism

Communism is a form of government described in the mid-1800s by German philosophers Karl Marx and Friedrich Engels. Communism called for workers to unite and become the owners of factories, farms, or other businesses. Marx believed a revolution was needed before this could happen. Violence might be necessary to achieve their goal.

Karl Marx

In 1917, Vladimir Lenin formed the Communist Party in Russia. It led a revolution that overthrew the czar, or emperor. Unfortunately, Communism did not result in a better life or more freedom for the people of Russia. When Lenin died, Joseph Stalin took over what was then called the Soviet Union. Stalin killed millions of people who disagreed with him. As head of the Communist Party, he was as power hungry as the czars had been. The Soviet Union lasted until 1991 when it broke up into many countries. The largest is again called Russia. It is no longer a Communist country, but still lacks many democratic freedoms.

Friedrich Engels

Studying was not nearly as important to Pete as working for a cause. At meetings everyone talked about changing the world. His grades suffered, he lost his scholarship, and Pete had to drop out of Harvard at nineteen.

So now what was Pete going to do? One thing was certain. He needed to find work he would enjoy. However, first he decided to take a summer bicycle vacation through the countryside in New York and New England. He didn't have money to go to restaurants or stay in hotels. But Pete liked to draw. Maybe he could earn a living as an artist.

He painted watercolor pictures of farmers' homes or barns. He didn't charge any money for his paintings. Instead he traded his art for meals and permission to sleep in the farmers' barns.

When summer ended, Pete moved into an apartment in New York City with his oldest brother, Charles, and his brother's wife, Inez. One day, Inez dared Pete to perform music on the street.

Pete plucked up his nerve, but all he made after three hours of singing was seventy-five cents.

Pete was a good writer and tried to get a job working for a newspaper. He had no luck getting hired. But he didn't give up on his music and got a few small paying jobs. Then Pete was introduced to a musician named Huddie Ledbetter. Huddie was an African American from Louisiana who liked to be called Lead Belly. The way Lead Belly sang and played his twelve-string guitar amazed Pete.

Huddie Ledbetter

Pete still wasn't sure he could earn enough money. Then a friend asked him to play his music in a traveling puppet group. It wouldn't pay much, but Pete thought it would be fun. The job lasted through the summer.

Alan Lomax was another very helpful friend. Alan was collecting folk and blues music for Library of Congress.

Both Alan and his father, John, would go out in the fields and sometimes even to prisons to hear the music of country folks. What interested them most was the music of African Americans.

Alan Lomax

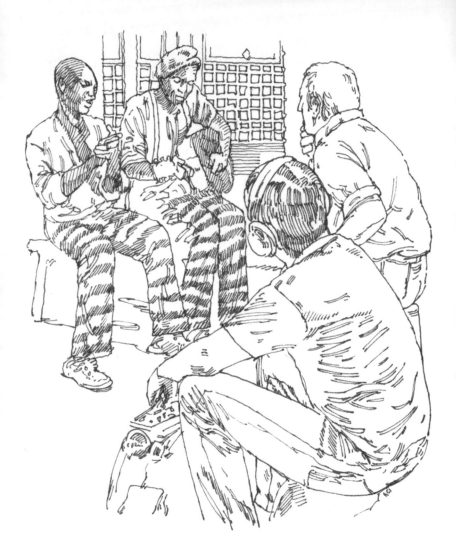

Without the Lomaxes, Americans might never have known about songs that had been passed down since the time of slavery.

The Library of Congress

The Library of Congress is America's greatest library. Located in Washington, DC, it takes up three buildings with 838 miles of bookshelves. It stores more than 158 million items. Besides rare books, there are maps, musical tapes and records, movies, and the digital information we use today. Much of this incredible information can be viewed or listened to on the Library of Congress website.

Alan gave Pete a job in Washington, DC, helping write down the words and music to songs for the Library of Congress. Pete earned only fifteen dollars a week. But he learned a lot of new folk songs and a lot about the struggles of African Americans in the South.

In 1940, Pete got a big break. Alan asked him to perform at a concert in New York City. It was to raise money for poor farmworkers in the western states. They had moved from the Midwest, where there had been terrible dust storms.

The concert took place in a big Broadway theater. Pete's turn came long after more famous folk singers had performed. Finally onstage, Pete got so nervous he forgot some words to the song. Pete later recalled: "I played and sang it terribly . . . My fingers froze up on me."

It was a rocky start. But backstage, Pete was introduced to a skinny singer from Oklahoma. He was wearing a cowboy hat and boots and his name was Woody Guthrie. Woody liked the way Pete played banjo. The two became close friends.

It was another life-changing moment for Pete Seeger. His music would never be the same after he met Woody.

Woody Guthrie

Woody Guthrie was seven years older than Pete. He grew up poor and made his name performing on a radio show in California. He wrote his own songs—often songs about the hard times of poor people.

Perhaps his most famous song is "This Land Is Your Land." It praises the beauty of the United States "from the redwood forests to the Gulfstream waters." But the last part of the song wasn't often played on radio or taught in schools. Those words shared the message that poor people

should have the same chance as the rich to enjoy the beauty of America.

Woody asked Pete to drive to Texas with him. On the way, the friends played for anyone who would listen. They played in small restaurants or bars for tips. Sometimes they got a good meal instead of money. Pete helped Woody write the words and music for two new songs: "66 Highway Blues" and "Union Maid." Both songs were recorded later.

Woody's Later Years

In 1954, doctors told Woody that he had an incurable disease. The illness is now called Huntington's Disease, and scientists still have not found a cure. Woody could no longer perform. He spent a lot of time in hospitals until his death in 1967 at age fifty-five.

During his years in the hospital, a new generation of folk singers discovered Woody's music. Called "Woody's Children," they included Bob Dylan; Joan Baez; Peter, Paul, and Mary; Judy Collins; Phil Ochs; and Arlo Guthrie (Woody's son). Musicians today are still listening to and learning from Woody Guthrie's music.

Woody and his son Arlo

Neither Woody nor Pete was interested in fame or getting rich. They thought it was more important for songs to tell the truth about the suffering Americans faced during the Great Depression.

Woody taught Pete so much. Besides his musical talent, he had a sharp sense of humor and could tell jokes and stories that held an audience's attention. Later Pete wrote, "I learned so many different things from Woody that I can hardly count them."

Soon Pete started to travel on his own after learning the ropes from Woody. He didn't own a car so he hitchhiked. He also learned how to "ride the rails," which meant sneaking onto freight trains. Although it was dangerous hiding out in a boxcar, it was a free way to travel.

On the trains, Pete met hobos. They were men without homes, jobs, or much money.

On one train, Pete heard that a policeman was waiting at the next station. He liked to shoot at anyone "riding the rails." Pete jumped off just before the train pulled in. When he landed, his banjo broke. Pete bought a five-dollar guitar to use until he could save enough for a new banjo.

The Almanac Singers

Woody   Millard Lampell   Lee Hays   Pete

Once back in New York City, Pete, Lee Hays, and Millard Lampell formed a group called the Almanac Singers. They wanted their music to help American workers and the union cause. Woody Guthrie also joined the group.

American Unions

In the early 1900s, many American workers joined groups called unions to demand fair treatment and better pay. If their demands were not met, a union might have members go on strike—to stop working. Some of the early powerful unions were for steel workers, auto workers, and railroad workers. The union movement was led by people willing to go to jail for their beliefs.

By 1937, about seven million Americans had joined a union. In 1938, President Franklin D. Roosevelt passed a law to help unions and workers get fair treatment.

The Almanac Singers—including Pete—belonged to the Communist Party USA. The party believed in the union cause. The Almanac Singers wrote songs and gave concerts to show their support. Both the Communist Party USA and the Almanac Singers also worked to end the unjust treatment of African Americans.

CHAPTER 3
Love and War

Pete's life wasn't only music and politics. He started going to square dances in New York City, where in 1939 he met a beautiful woman. She was named Toshi Ohta and was Japanese American. Toshi believed in the same causes Pete did. But Pete was so busy with his music and traveling that he and Toshi didn't start dating until 1942.

Toshi Ohta

It wasn't long before Pete knew Toshi was the woman he wanted to marry. He took her to meet his father and stepmother in Washington, DC. That's where he broke the news that they were engaged.

But their wedding had to wait. America had entered World War II in December of 1941 after the Japanese bombed Pearl Harbor in Hawaii. Pete was drafted to join the army the following year. Toshi told him, "I'll wait for you."

It was difficult for Pete to leave Toshi. He spent his first year in the army learning to repair B-24 bomber airplanes in Mississippi.

He graduated second in his class. All of Pete's classmates were getting sent overseas to fight in Europe or in the Pacific Islands. Pete couldn't understand why he was left behind.

Years later, Pete learned that the army had opened his mail, including letters from Toshi. The army leaders didn't trust a soldier with a sweetheart whose father was originally from Japan.

After six months in Mississippi, Pete asked for a short time off to marry Toshi. The wedding took place in a little church in New York City on July 20, 1943. Pete didn't have enough money to give Toshi a wedding ring, so she wore her grandmother's.

She also paid the two dollars for their wedding license.

Soon Pete got transferred to Maryland. Now he could visit Toshi more often. One night Pete was playing guitar with some other soldiers.

Even after lights out, they kept playing in the latrine—the bathroom area. About forty guys stood in shower stalls or sat on sinks and toilet seats so that they could listen. Pete later wrote that if anyone asked him where he made some of the best music in his life, he would reply, "In the latrine."

In 1944, Pete was finally sent to the Pacific. The officers on board the ship saw how Pete could best serve his country. He was put in charge of entertainment at a hospital for wounded soldiers.

In the summer of 1944, Pete received a letter from Toshi with thrilling news. She had given birth to a little boy named Peter. The proud new

papa passed out cigars to his army buddies.

Sadly, Pete and Toshi's joy was short-lived. Months later, Pete received another letter. Baby Peter had died from a birth problem that doctors could not fix. Poor Toshi. Poor Pete. Thousands of miles apart, they could not even comfort each other. How terrible that Pete Seeger never got to see his first-born child.

World War II finally ended when the Japanese surrendered on September 2, 1945. The United States had dropped an atom bomb on two cities in Japan, which convinced that country to give up the fighting. Pete had to stay overseas until December. Unfortunately, peace did not really come to the world when the war ended. A new kind of war—the "Cold War"—arrived. There were no actual battles, but it was still a very dangerous time.

Pete and Toshi were overjoyed to be together after such a long time apart. At first, the young couple lived in Toshi's parents' apartment in New York City. They were thrilled with the arrival of baby Daniel on Labor Day of 1946.

There was more celebration for the Seeger family when a daughter named Mika was born in 1948.

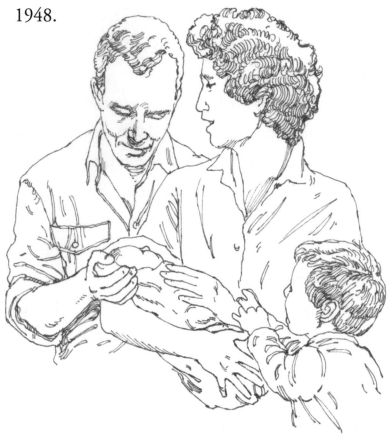

Pete, however, didn't get to spend much time with his family. He earned twenty-five dollars a week writing a folk music newsletter.

The Cold War

The Soviet Union and the United States fought together in World War II. But after the war, the two nations, known as the superpowers, became enemies. The United States wanted to prevent the Soviet Union from spreading Communism to the rest of the world. A cold war began—one with no soldiers actually firing at one another. But both countries now had atom bombs—bombs so powerful that just one could destroy an entire city. During the Cold War, the world lived in fear that one side might use atomic weapons. The Cold War lasted for forty-five years until the collapse of the Soviet Union in 1991.

SOVIET UNION

EUROPE

Then at night, Pete played in sing-along groups called hootenannies. Friends and neighbors would pay thirty-five cents to listen to great folk music, often in somebody's apartment.

The politics of Pete and his friends scared the United States government. The FBI started to spy on folk singers at hootenannies. Why?

Because many had been or still were members of the Communist Party USA. People connected to that group were called "Reds." Their phones were tapped—the government listened to their calls—in an effort to find out if they were disloyal to the United States. The American Constitution says citizens can belong to the political party of their choice. But now the Red Scare—the fear of Communism spreading—made people in the government do things they should not have.

Pete believed in democracy, the American way of government. In 1948, he worked to help elect a man running for president. His name was Henry Wallace. Wallace had been the vice president under Franklin Delano Roosevelt from 1941 to 1945.

Henry Wallace

He supported civil rights for African Americans and other causes Pete believed in. Toshi often brought their new baby daughter, Mika, to concerts Pete gave for Wallace. But Wallace didn't get very many votes. Harry Truman was elected

Harry Truman

president. Even the new president was accused of not being hard enough on communism.

It was a dangerous time in America to stand up for your beliefs. But Pete Seeger was never a man to remain silent.

In 1949, Pete decided to perform in a concert with Paul Robeson.

Paul Robeson

Robeson was among the greatest singers and actors of the time. He was also African American.

The concert was to raise money for civil rights groups. The lives of African Americans in the South had improved very little since the Civil War. They were treated as second-class citizens.

The performance was to be held outdoors near Peekskill, New York, just over an hour's drive north of New York City. A group called the Ku Klux Klan, which hated blacks, Jews, and Communists, had lots of members in the Peekskill area.

With the Klan's help, people at the concert were attacked with clubs, brass knuckles, and rocks. The performance was stopped. The attackers lit a cross set up nearby—cross burnings were popular with the Ku Klux Klan in the South.

But Paul Robeson, Pete Seeger, and others refused to be silenced. They decided to perform the following week. The Ku Klux Klan promised to be back as well.

Close to twenty thousand people came to hear Paul Robeson and Pete Seeger sing. Toshi and her father decided to attend with little Danny and Mika.

Everything seemed peaceful. However, a violent mob was waiting for the concert to end. When it did, people threw rocks at cars leaving the concert. One rock crashed through the window of the Seeger family's Jeep. Toshi's father lay over little Danny. Pieces of broken glass stuck in the child's skin and hair.

More than 140 people were injured by the
attackers. Paul Robeson and Pete Seeger were lucky
to escape alive. There had been policemen at the
event. Did they help? No! They let it happen. It
was an ugly moment. Even in the Northern states
like New York, many were against equal rights for
black people.

CHAPTER 4
Little House on the Hudson

Life was certainly not easy for Pete and his family. However, a wonderful thing happened in 1949. Pete and Toshi wanted to leave New York City and raise Danny and Mika in the country. They didn't have enough money to buy a house. But with loans from family and friends, they bought seventeen and a half acres of mountainside woods in Beacon, New York. Their land overlooked the Hudson River.

Pete and Toshi had land now. What they didn't have was a house! So Pete went to the New York Public Library and looked up "log cabin." He was going to build one himself!

Amazingly, the cabin's foundation was finished by summer's end. Pete, Toshi, and the kids slept in tents under the stars. When colder weather came,

Toshi and the children stayed with her parents while Pete and friends went on building.

Pete was thrilled when the log cabin was finished. He had always wanted to live close to nature. Toshi wanted the same life, too, though it wasn't easy. There was no electricity or running water in the early years. Toshi carried buckets of water from the nearby stream to use for cooking over a fire or for washing clothes and diapers. She did all this work with a toddler at her side and a baby on her hip.

As for Pete, he was often in New York City looking for work. In 1948, Pete had helped start a new singing group with four members—one girl and three guys. One was his good friend Lee Hays from the Almanac Singers. Their voices blended perfectly together. They called themselves the Weavers.

At first, the Weavers played mostly at parties and didn't seem to be on the road to success. Pete

had never cared about fame and mainly hoped that their music would help the cause of American workers. Yet with their very first record, the Weavers became the number one singing group in America.

The Weavers figured out how to make old-fashioned folk music sound new to audiences. Some fans had never heard folk songs before. The record companies didn't know how to describe the Weavers' style. Pete later answered that question by saying: "the important thing is a song, a good song, a true song. . . . Call it anything you want."

The Weavers' big break came at a club called the Village Vanguard in New York City around Christmas of 1949. Alan Lomax brought Carl Sandburg, one of America's greatest poets, to hear them.

Carl Sandburg

Afterward, Carl Sandburg wrote a newspaper review saying, "The Weavers are out of the grass roots of America. I salute them . . . When I hear America singing, the Weavers are there." Before long, crowds were packing the Village Vanguard.

In 1950, the Weavers made their first record. Back then, little records called forty-fives were

made with just two songs. They cost about a dollar. One side of the Weavers' forty-five featured "Goodnight Irene," a song made popular by Lead Belly. The other side featured a lively tune from Israel called "Tzena Tzena Tzena."

The Weavers sold more than a million copies of their record!

It was during his time with the Weavers that Pete decided to leave the Communist Party

J. Edgar Hoover

USA. He was now troubled by the way Communism had turned out in the Soviet Union. His change of heart, however, did not matter to powerful people in the government. Two men in particular— J. Edgar Hoover, who was the director of the FBI, and Joe McCarthy, a senator from Wisconsin— wanted to ruin the careers of anyone in the United States who had ever belonged to the Communist Party.

The FBI paid Harvey Matusow, who was a former Communist Party

Joe McCarthy

member, to spy on folk singers like Pete. Matusow did this by pretending to be a fan of the Weavers' music. He later admitted making up stories to please the FBI and Joe McCarthy. But his spying did a lot of damage to Pete and others.

Harvey Matusow

The FBI sent lists of names to the big companies who sponsored radio and TV shows. No one on the lists would be hired to appear on the shows. This was called "blacklisting."

By 1952, the blacklist brought the success of the Weavers to a crashing halt. They had been offered their own TV show but the contract was torn up. Record stores stopped selling their music. Concerts were canceled. So the Weavers disbanded.

Pete was on his own again.

Senator Joe McCarthy

From 1950 to 1954, Republican Senator Joe McCarthy headed a Senate Committee to investigate suspected Communists in America. J. Edgar Hoover, head of the FBI, worked closely with McCarthy. Thousands of people—many in the entertainment fields—lost their jobs. Many went to prison.

McCarthy's investigations were shown on TV. This was something new, and Americans did not like what they saw. This was not how democracy was supposed to work. Finally, President Dwight Eisenhower got other senators to speak out against McCarthy. McCarthy lost his job in the Senate in 1954. He died three years later of alcoholism at the age of forty-eight.

CHAPTER 5
Pete on Trial

In 1955, a big black car drove up to the Seegers' house in Beacon. A man handed Pete a subpoena (say: sub-PEE-na). A subpoena is a document ordering a person to appear at court. Pete was not being put on trial. Not yet. But he had to speak before a government committee known as HUAC.

It stood for the House Un-American Activities Committee.

McCarthy was gone from the Senate, but in the House of Representatives, members still were hunting down American Communists. Their main targets were entertainers, writers, musicians, and artists. HUAC wanted to make sure that Communist ideas would not appear in the movies Americans watched, the books they read, or the music they heard.

Pete's friends had been investigated by HUAC. He was not surprised that his turn had come.

Some people chose to make a deal with HUAC. When asked for information about others, including friends who might be Communists, they gave it. This was known as "naming names." It was a way to avoid going to jail for contempt of Congress.

Toshi helped find a lawyer to handle Pete's

case. He understood that Pete would never name names. Instead, he advised Pete to refuse to answer anything at the hearing that could make him look guilty. It is perfectly legal to do this. It is called "pleading the Fifth Amendment."

It was the safest way for Pete to avoid going to jail.

But Pete wouldn't take his lawyer's advice. Didn't pleading the Fifth make a person look guilty? And Pete wasn't guilty of anything. He was a loyal American who had served his country during World War II.

The HUAC hearing was held in New York City. Pete was asked whether he had sung at events supporting the Communist Party. He felt HUAC had no right to pry into his political beliefs even though by this time he had left the Communist Party USA. He told HUAC that freedom of speech and opinion, just like freedom of religion, were rights given to every

American by the Constitution. He said the hearing was "improper"—not right. And he wasn't going to answer any of the questions.

When Pete left the hearing, he told friends, "I still feel I committed no wrong, and that my children will not feel ashamed of me in future years."

Because he had not cooperated at the HUAC hearing, Pete now faced trial. And if he was found guilty, he would be put behind bars.

Pete Seeger was willing to give up his freedom to protect his right to believe and say whatever he wanted.

The trial was delayed for years. In the meantime, Pete remained on the blacklist.

Good-paying music jobs were impossible to find. So Pete played for children at summer camps and in school assemblies. He played college concerts. He worked nonstop and he loved it. At the performances, kids heard Pete's music and became lifelong fans.

Toshi was now Pete's manager. Pete took every job Toshi could find. That meant even less time at home, where the family had grown to include a baby girl named Tinya, born in 1956. One year, Pete played in almost every state and also in Canada.

Finally, in 1961, Pete was brought to trial. The charge was contempt of Congress. That meant he had refused to help HUAC. Pete was sentenced to a year and one day in jail.

A large crowd gathered outside the courtroom to protest the court's decision.

Pete spent a few hours in jail before his lawyer got him released. A second trial was set up to allow Pete another chance to prove his innocence.

Fortunately, by 1961, many Americans realized that the blacklist and HUAC were wrong. In fact, former President Harry Truman said HUAC was "the most un-American thing in the country today."

The second trial cost the Seegers a great deal of money but was worth it. In 1962, the government dropped its court case against Pete Seeger. Not only was it a tremendous relief for the Seegers personally, it was a sign that the United States was changing.

CHAPTER 6
We Shall Overcome

During the early sixties, folk music became incredibly popular on college campuses. Songs that Pete helped write or discover —"Where Have All the Flowers Gone," "If I Had a Hammer," "Guantanamera" from Cuba, and "Wimoweh" from Africa—became huge hits. And now that he didn't have to worry about going to prison, Pete was ready to speak out through songs in support of the growing civil rights movement.

Years earlier, Pete had met Martin Luther King Jr. in Tennessee at the Highlander Folk School.

Martin Luther King Jr.

Blacks and whites lived and studied there together.

At Highlander, Pete heard an old song from the days of slavery. It was called "I'll Be Alright." Pete made some small changes in the words and the song became known as "We Shall Overcome." Soon it was sung at almost every gathering of Americans protesting laws against blacks in the South.

Between 1962 and 1965, Pete and Toshi joined Dr. King on the Freedom Marches in Southern states. The marches were shown on TV and drew attention to the cause of civil rights. Marchers put their lives at risk. Police used dogs and fire hoses to attack them. But they would not fight back because they believed in peaceful, non-violent protests.

Pete's job was to inspire crowds with his music. During a concert in Mississippi, he learned that the bodies of three civil rights workers had been discovered nearby. They were murdered by the Ku Klux Klan. The audience was stunned by the horrible news and wept openly. Pete closed his performance by saying, "We must sing 'We Shall Overcome' now.

The three boys would not have wanted us to weep, but to sing and understand this song."

On August 28, 1963, a quarter of a million people, white and black, took part in a March on Washington. They marched to demand better jobs and equal rights for African Americans. Martin Luther King Jr. addressed the entire nation with his "I Have a Dream" speech,

which was also broadcast on TV. In addition to other speakers, there were songs performed by Marian Anderson; Mahalia Jackson; Joan Baez; Bob Dylan; Peter, Paul, and Mary; and Odetta.

Lyndon Johnson

The March on Washington brought real change. In the next two years, President Lyndon Johnson got Congress to pass important laws—the Civil Rights Act of 1964 and the Voting Rights Act of 1965.

Was Pete Seeger at the March on Washington? It seems like exactly the sort of event he would have loved being part of. However, he was not there. In fact, he was not even in the United States.

For a long time, Pete and Toshi had thought of taking their children to see other parts of the world. They wanted them to see how people lived in places most Americans knew little about.

So in August of 1963, they flew to Australia. In the next ten months, they visited fourteen countries on four continents. Toshi filmed the music and dances of the countries they visited.

Her movie is now part of the Library of Congress film collection. Pete gave concerts to pay expenses and to make enough money to get the family to their next stop. In India, Pete performed before twenty thousand people. Millions more listened to the concert on the radio.

CHAPTER 7
Give Peace a Chance

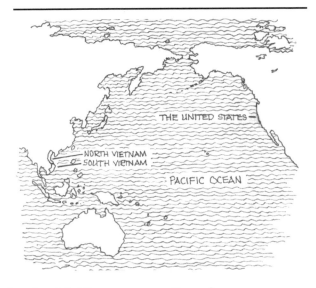

As the 1960s wore on, Pete Seeger was among the many Americans who were angry about a war thousands of US soldiers were fighting halfway around the world. Vietnam, a small country in southeast Asia, was split into two parts. The northern half of the country was ruled by a Communist government.

President Lyndon Johnson sent US troops to the area to keep the southern half of the country from becoming Communist. Many people, Pete among them, felt that the United States had no business deciding the affairs of countries on the other side of the globe.

Pete wrote a new song he called "Waist Deep in the Big Muddy." The song told a story about an American officer giving foolish orders to his soldiers. It didn't mention the Vietnam War. But it did ask questions about a war that made no sense.

Once again, Pete got in trouble for speaking his mind. *The Smothers Brothers Comedy Hour* was a hit TV show on CBS. In 1967, Pete was invited on the show to sing that song. It was a big moment for him. The blacklist had kept him from performing on television for years.

But the TV show was pre-recorded. And

afterward CBS decided to cut Pete's protest song from the program.

The Smothers Brothers were furious. They insisted that Pete return and do the number. He did. Was this the end of the uproar? No. One year later CBS decided to fire the Smothers Brothers and cancel the popular comedy show.

In the late 1960s, the protest movement against the war grew even stronger. Pete continued to sing and speak out for an end to the fighting. In Washington, DC, at a war protest in 1969,

Pete led half a million people in John Lennon's song "Give Peace a Chance."

American troops finally left Vietnam in 1973. More than fifty-eight thousand American soldiers gave their lives in the Vietnam War. It is estimated that several million Vietnamese lost their lives; over half of those who died were not soldiers. The bloodshed did not stop Vietnam from becoming one country that remains Communist to this day.

CHAPTER 8
The Clearwater

Vietnam was on the other side of the globe from Beacon, New York, where, by the late sixties, the Seegers had been living for twenty years. And in those twenty years, Pete and Toshi had seen changes—bad changes—in the natural world outside their door.

Pete loved to take his family and friends sailing on the Hudson River in his small sailboat.

However, the water was filthy. There was floating garbage in the water. Fish were dying and the river contained dangerous chemicals dumped by factories.

A friend showed Pete an old book called *Sloops of the Hudson*. This book told the history of the majestic Hudson River boats of the 1800s. The book had beautiful illustrations. They captured Pete's imagination. An idea was born. What if New Yorkers could see how important the Hudson River was by sailing aboard one of these sloops? If they came to know the river, wouldn't more people want to clean it up?

Just as he had once decided he needed to live in a log cabin, Pete now decided he needed to build a sloop. He couldn't build it himself, at least not all by himself; instead, he would raise the money to have a sloop made. He would need a lot of people's help, so Pete and Toshi founded the Clearwater Organization.

In 1968, some New York City shipbuilders told Pete it would cost about $300,000 to build the kind of sloop he wanted. That amount would equal over $2 million today. Pete knew that price would be too expensive. Then Harvey Gamage, a shipbuilder in Maine, offered to build the sloop for under $150,000. That was half the price of the other shipbuilder. Many people still thought Pete's project was crazy. But Toshi set up concerts where Pete and others performed, sometimes three or four times a day, to raise money.

Nearing his fiftieth birthday, Pete was determined to help him. So off he went to South Bristol, Maine. He grew a beard for the first time and felt a surge of new energy. Pete always loved hard physical work. He also learned some new folk songs sung by sailors in the old days.

About nine months later, on June 27, 1969, the *Clearwater* made its first voyage. Toshi and others arranged for concerts to be held where the *Clearwater* docked on the way to the Hudson River. Its first stop was Portland, Maine. The very first voyage, which ended in New York

City's harbor, raised $27,000 for cleaning up the Hudson River.

The Clearwater Organization is probably Pete Seeger's most practical gift to America. In 1969, he promised his teenage daughter Tinya that one day she and her friends would be able to swim in the Hudson. The water would be that clean! It seemed like a far-fetched promise, but with the help of many volunteers, Pete and Toshi Seeger made it come true.

The *Clearwater* drew more people to the Hudson. At concerts, they signed up to work on passing laws to stop companies and individuals from dumping waste in the Hudson. Through Clearwater programs, New Yorkers learned about chemicals and pesticides that killed fish and polluted the water. A major federal law called the Clean Water Act was passed in 1972. States like New York could now fine companies for polluting rivers.

By the mid-1980s, people noticed that the river was much cleaner. More people could swim in much of the Hudson. Today, Pete's hometown of Beacon features a rainbow-colored pool that floats in the Hudson River for summer swimming.

Like the Clearwater Organization, the Beacon Sloop Club looks after the Hudson River. Pete and Toshi were Club members and loved to attend the monthly potluck suppers and hootenannies.

Since 1969, over half a million people have sailed on the *Clearwater*. Most passengers are children who learn how to keep the Hudson clean for the future. Every year the organization holds a two-day event called the Clearwater Festival, which draws thousands of concertgoers. The bands and performers share a vision of saving planet Earth for future generations. All because of Pete Seeger!

CHAPTER 9
American Hero

In 1979, Pete turned sixty. He had started out in folk music as a teenager. Now he was a grandfather. Younger musicians looked up to him.

The bad times of the blacklist were behind him. During the 1980s, Pete joined Arlo Guthrie and his band for many sold-out performances,

including concerts at the famous Carnegie Hall in New York City.

Besides performing, Pete continued to write, mostly about folk music. He wrote more than thirty books. A story song Pete loved to perform at family concerts called "Abiyoyo" was made into a much-loved children's picture book.

Of course, all of Pete's work was possible only with Toshi's support. In interviews, Pete called Toshi the real hero (and brains) of the Seeger family. Pete wrote that without Toshi, "the world would not turn nor the sun shine."

The man who almost went to prison for being "un-American" was now seen as a national hero. In 1994, President Clinton awarded seventy-five-year-old Pete the National Medal of Arts for both his music and his work for so many causes. Weeks later Pete received the Kennedy Center Honor,

again presented by President Clinton. Clinton's words describing Pete's life rang true: "Some artists make musical history. Pete Seeger made history with his music."

Two years later, Pete was chosen as an honorary member of the Rock and Roll Hall of Fame.

Rock and Roll? How could that be, when Pete was a folk singer?

The reason was that Pete's song "Turn! Turn! Turn!" had been a number one hit for a rock band named The Byrds. When Roger McGuinn, leader of the group, was a child growing up in the 1950s, he had listened to Pete perform the song. Rock musicians understood how folk musicians—especially Pete Seeger—had influenced their music.

Pete's voice lost strength as he entered his eighties. It gave him joy when his audience joined in to make up for this difficulty. He thought singing together with others was what counted, particularly songs speaking out for what was right. Pete Seeger thought songs could actually change people and make the world a better place.

"Old Pete," as he liked to call himself, earned Grammy Awards for Best Traditional Folk Album with *Pete* and *At 89*.

Bruce Springsteen, along with twelve other musicians, recorded *We Shall Overcome: The Seeger Sessions*. The album was a tribute to Pete's music. Bruce's concert tour of *The Seeger Sessions* packed stadiums throughout the world.

Pete accepted the recognition with modesty. Fame and attention, however, were never Pete's goals. Pete didn't want to be worshipped as a hero or superstar—he wanted all Americans to realize they had the power to accomplish great things. And something as simple as a song could help do it.

In 2008, Barack Obama was elected the first black president of the United States. He asked Pete to perform with Bruce Springsteen at the Lincoln Memorial in Washington, DC, two days before he took office. Pete's grandson Tao

Rodríguez-Seeger, joined them singing Woody Guthrie's "This Land Is Your Land." Pete made sure that all the verses, including the ones that spoke out against poverty, were sung. Millions of Americans enjoyed the moment on television.

Tao Rodríguez-Seeger   Pete Seeger   Bruce Springsteen

Pete turned down an invitation to a special party after the concert. Why? He wanted to get back to Beacon to rehearse songs with children at the elementary school there. For Pete, playing music with the kids in his hometown was more important than a party with celebrities. In 2010, Pete recorded *Tomorrow's Children* with

Beacon students who called themselves the Rivertown Kids. The album won that year's Grammy Award for Best Musical Album for Children.

The Beacon High School named their new auditorium for Pete and Toshi in 2013. For Toshi, .the honor was long overdue. Her behind-the-scenes work had given the world so much, and her sacrifices made Pete's work possible.

Sadly, Toshi died on July 9 that summer at age ninety-one. The Seegers were only eleven days away from celebrating their seventieth wedding anniversary.

Pete's life was nearing an end as well. There would be a few more concerts, including a final Carnegie Hall performance with Arlo Guthrie. He still loved to perform! What Pete enjoyed most at age ninety-four was being at home with his daughter Tinya, visits from Dan and Mika, six grandchildren, and one great-grandson, and his many friends.

In December of 2013, Pete started making plans for a special march in Beacon to celebrate Martin Luther King Jr. Day. It was to take place on January 20, 2014. But by the holiday, when more than three hundred people gathered to march and sing, Pete was not among them. He wasn't feeling well. The parade went on anyway. Everyone understood that Pete would be counting on them to keep working for freedom.

The next day, Pete entered a New York City hospital. For six days, a steady stream of close friends joined Pete's children and grandchildren to show their love and say good-bye to the beloved singer. At his bedside, they held hands in a circle and sang songs or told stories. Pete Seeger died peacefully on January 27, 2014.

Pete Seeger left behind more than a lot of wonderful music. His message to the world can be summed up in one word: participate.

He wanted everyone to make their own music and sing with one another. He proved that small acts of kindness and bravery can add up and make a big difference if people stand together.

These words from a song written by Noel Paul Stookey of Peter, Paul, and Mary explain the magic of Pete Seeger:

"There always was this moment
Kinda hard to understand
When the music became bigger than the man."

Timeline of Pete Seeger's Life

1919	Born on May 3 in New York City
1927	Parents, Charles and Constance, divorce
1932	Learns banjo at boarding school
1938	Drops out of Harvard
1939	Meets Toshi Ohta
1940	Meets Woody Guthrie
1941	Helps start his first musical group, the Almanac Singers
1942	Joins the US Army
1943	Pete and Toshi marry
1949	Begins work on family log cabin in Beacon, New York
	Ku Klux Klan riots at Peekskill, New York, concert
1950	The Weavers record number one hit "Goodnight Irene"
1955	HUAC (congressional committee) investigates Pete
1962	Government drops the case against Pete
1967	Appears on *Smothers Brothers* TV show (first TV appearance since being blacklisted)
1969	*Clearwater* sloop is launched
1994	President Clinton honors Pete with National Medal of Arts and Kennedy Center Honor
2009	Sings at concert celebrating President Obama's inauguration
2014	Dies on January 27 at age ninety-four

Timeline of the World

1918	World War I ends
1922	Communists in Russia form the Soviet Union
1929	The stock market crashes and the Great Depression begins
1940	Woody Guthrie writes "This Land Is Your Land"
1941	Japan bombs Pearl Harbor, and America enters World War II
1945	World War II ends
1949	Mao Tse-tung forms Communist government in China
1950–1953	America fights Communists in the Korean War
1955	Montgomery bus boycott begins
1963	Dr. Martin Luther King Jr. gives "I Have a Dream" speech
1964	America increases bombing in the Vietnam War
1968	Dr. Martin Luther King Jr. assassinated
1970	First Earth Day celebrated
1973	American troops leave Vietnam
1980	Plan to build Con Edison power plant on the Hudson River is halted
1991	The Soviet Union collapses
2001	Terrorists attack the World Trade Center in New York and the Pentagon near Washington, DC
2009	Barack Obama begins the first of two terms as the first African American president of the United States

Bibliography

Brown, Jim. *Pete Seeger: The Power of Song.* Video recording. Santa Monica, CA: Weinstein Company Home Entertainment, 2008.

Brown, Jim. *The Weavers: Wasn't That a Time!* Video recording. Burbank, CA: Warner Reprise Video, 1992 (copyright 1981).

Cohen, Ronald D., and James Capaldi, eds. *The Pete Seeger Reader.* New York: Oxford University Press, 2014.

Dunaway, David King. *How Can I Keep from Singing?: The Ballad of Pete Seeger.* New York: Villard, 2008.

Seeger, Pete. *Pete Seeger: In His Own Words.* Boulder, CO: Paradigm Publishers, 2012.

Wilkinson, Alec. *The Protest Singer: An Intimate Portrait of Pete Seeger.* New York: Alfred A. Knopf, 2009.

Winkler, Alan M. *To Everything There Is a Season: Pete Seeger and the Power of Song.* New York: Oxford University Press, 2009.

WEBSITES

For more information about Pete Seeger and Clearwater
www.clearwater.org